When Life Speaks

You Speak Life!
Inspiration through Affirmations

Andrea L. Hines
FOREWORD BY TRACY "TRACYMAC" MCNEIL

Studio Griffin
A Publishing Company
www.studiogriffin.net

When Life Speaks. Copyright © 2018 Andrea L. Hines

All Rights Reserved. Printed in the United States of America. No part of this book may be used or reproduced in any manner whatsoever without written permission except in the case of brief quotations embodied in critical articles and reviews.

For information, contact:
Studio Griffin
A Publishing Company
studiogriffin@outlook.com
www.studiogriffin.net

Cover Design by Ruth E. Griffin
Image by © Tripp/Adobe

This book is licensed for your personal enjoyment only and may not be reproduced, transmitted or stored in whole or in part by any means including graphic, electronic or mechanical without expressed written consent of the author.

First Edition

ISBN-13: 978-1-954818-02-6

1 2 3 4 5 6 7 8 9 10

Dedication

Past… Present… Generations to come…

To my parents, Ernest and Anna Henson, who now peer over the balcony of heaven and witness the rich heritage they left on the earth.

To my daughter Audra Lynnette, and grandchildren Christian and Jazzmen, who are active participants in building the legacy I will leave behind.

My love and appreciation grow with every passing day.

Foreword

The day I met Andrea L. Hines, a sense of calm, elegance and wisdom entered into the room, and into my life, the moment she walked in. We met when she was seeking information about life coach certification. Not only has she become a certified life coach and an affiliate of TRACYMAC Solutions For Life Institute, but clients who are privileged to invest in the services of her coaching practice (C.L.A.S.S. Coaching and Consulting) experience the benefits that flow with ease from this incredible woman, mother, grandmother, friend, ordained elder, three-time author, brilliant poet, radio and talk show host and I dare not forget, IBM retiree. Andrea L. Hines is an undisputed treasure box of wisdom. She doesn't simply have wisdom. She *is* wisdom because she implements it. This, I can affirm.

We can't sleep on the need for and the power of wisdom. We can't ignore it when we see hashtags like #StayWoke, #MeToo or #TimesUp. They may be trending the "what's" going on, but what voices are qualified to express and be an example of the "how" to fix it or make a difference? This is where wisdom comes in and *Speaks Life*. As the world turns we see, in heavy rotation, on the news and on social media, how we are inundated with the negativity of politics, racism, sexism, religious indifference and the unfair treatment of our elderly, the weak and the poor. We see how the livelihoods of our families, personal and professional relationships, the effectiveness of the church and our communities is being shaken at the very core. This climate, if you allow it, can wreak havoc on your mind and body.

How do you silence the noise? Where can you find encouragement to be the change you want to see? It starts with how you see yourself. It begins with how you are encouraged and motivated on a daily basis. Because it is impossible to have a troubled mind and a whole soul. So, how do you ease your mind, calm our spirit and not become overwhelmed? What strategies can you use in bite-sized pieces that can keep you relevant and make a difference?

One of the ways is realizing that making a difference starts with using autosuggestion to encourage and motivate yourself. This is what affirmations are all about. Affirmations are foundational to genuine self-care. From my reading experience with this book, not only reading but choosing to digest and implement the affirmations given in this book, can help you reach within to receive the fuel you need to reach out. Affirmations promote continual self-discovery and self-advocacy. Neither are selfish, and both can give you the energy to be aware of what's going on and not be overwhelmed by it.

Use this resource, filled with relevant affirmations, to allow wisdom to give you peace and a plan. Allow it to help facilitate a peace that surpasses understanding for your life, mind and body. Use it to help you design a plan for how to offer your unique ways to create strategic and sustainable solutions. ***When Life Speaks*** is not about "you only" but supports "you first," which is where real solutions begin. I affirm that.

Peace and blessings,

Tracy "TracyMac" McNeil
CEO/ Senior Fellow
TRACYMAC Solutions for Life Coaching & Consulting Services

Preface

There are studies that suggest when you give praise, compliments and accolades, people try harder and work more diligently to achieve success or reach higher goals. Their attitude is better, and they are more productive overall. In reverse, negative words spoken over us have a negative impact on our lives. They can foster low self-confidence, diminish the desire to pursue your dreams and crush your creativity.

I know it may sound a little strange, but one of the greatest things I have come to realize is simply this: the most influential conversation I will ever have is the one I have with myself. I have discovered that even when someone speaks well of you, it carries very little weight unless you are also able to speak good things to you about you.

It seems we are more used to negative speech than we are positive affirmations. What do you think would change in your life if you made a conscious effort to change your speech and remove the negativity? What would happen if you earnestly acted as if you believed that death and life are in the power of the tongue and adjusted your language? What would you say differently if you were convinced you could have what you speak? What if you didn't just repeat Proverbs 18:21, or say you believed it, but you actually began to change your speech habits to plant positive seeds and fill the atmosphere with affirmations of hope and all things encouraging? What if you said, "I am at my ideal weight," rather than saying, "I'm not going to be fat anymore?" How about saying, "I walk in a realm of profound prosperity," instead of saying, "I'm not going to be broke anymore." If your words have power, what will you give them power to do? What will you give them power to bring into existence? I can tell you this: your faith will begin to rise, expectation will be activated, and your strength will be renewed.

You may have to make a switch in order to enjoy the power of the positive because negativity seems to be second nature. It may not be easy, and it might take a little more work than you envisioned. The good news is, now you have help. I have compiled thirty-one affirmations to take you through the month speaking life with boldness and authority. Read them aloud. Commit some lines to memory if you choose. Note pages have also been included for you to develop your own affirmations in and for a specific situation or circumstance you may be facing. You may find one sentence that resonates with you. You may find an entire affirmation that gives you strength. Perhaps you want to pull a line from one and add it to confessions from another to create just what you need. Whatever you choose to do, build your words of life and let them do what they are designed to do, empower you so that when life speaks, you speak life.

affirm
af·firm
ə-fûrm

v.

1. To state positively; assert to be true.
2. To declare support for or belief in.

affirmation
af·fir·ma·tion
ăf′ər-mā′shən

n.

1. The act of affirming or the state of being affirmed; assertion.
2. Something declared to be true; a positive statement or judgment.
3. A statement intended to provide encouragement, emotional support, or motivation.

declare
de·clare
dih-klair

v.

1. To make known or state clearly.
2. To state emphatically: he declared that the allegation was a lie.

decree
de.cree
dih-kree

v.

1. To command, ordain, or decide by decree.

Proverbs 18:21

Death and life are in the power of the tongue: and they that love it shall eat the fruit thereof. (*King James Version*)

Words kill, words give life; they're either poison or fruit—you choose. (*The Message Bible*)

What you say can preserve life or destroy it; so you must accept the consequences of your words. (*Good News Translation*)

Words can bring death or life! Talk too much, and you will eat everything you say. (*Contemporary English Version*)

Job 22:28

Thou shalt also decree a thing, and it shall be established unto thee: and the light shall shine upon thy ways. (*King James Version*)

You'll decide what you want and it will happen; your life will be bathed in light. (*The Message Bible*)

You will succeed in all you do, and light will shine on your path. (*Good News Translation*)

You will also decide and decree a thing, and it will be established for you; And the light [of God's favor] will shine upon your ways. (*The Amplified Bible*)

YOU have the power to change YOUr world.

Contents

Alignment	1
Assignment	2
Because I'm His	3
Celebrating Me	4
Character Traits	5
Chosen	6
Confession of the Extraordinary	7
Connection	8
Essential to the Equation	9
Expansion	10
Forgiveness	11
Game Plan	12
Health is Mine	13
I Am a Gift	14
Income and Increase	15
Lessons Learned	16
Love Is	17
My Identity	18
My Path	19
Predestinated	20

Prosperity Plan	21
Ready to Receive	22
Right Relationships	23
Setting the Day in Motion	24
Submitted to Him	25
This is the Day	26
Thoughts	27
Transformation	28
Traveling Light	29
Turnaround	30
Whose I Am	31
Journal Pages	33
Acknowledgments	67
About the Author	69
Find the Author Online	72
Also Available from the Author	73

When Life Speaks

You Speak Life!
Inspiration through Affirmations

Alignment

I keep my mind clear of clutter.
My discernment is vibrating on a higher frequency and
I differentiate between what is fake and fallible
from what is actual and authentic.
I move through the days keenly aware
of the things that rob me of my productivity
and I adjust accordingly.
I continually plan for success
with the flexibility that enables me to
perceive opportunities and open doors,
then react with wisdom.
Each day I expect the best outcomes
in my situations and circumstances.
I declare and decree
this is my set time.
I am prepared, and I am ready to receive.

Assignments

There is something specific
that I have been assigned to accomplish
and I declare and decree
my assignments will be completed in excellence.
I am delivered from unrealistic expectations.
I recognize what has a positive impact
on the achievement of my goals.
Therefore, I am open for solid suggestions,
wise counsel, and constructive correction.
I embrace those things that lead to positive behavior;
all the while understanding what is,
and is not, within my control.
Victories, great and small, are an acknowledgement
that I am fulfilling purpose.
I am a unique individual. I have unique assignments.
I have unique solutions.
I declare and decree
as I engage in self-examination and self-discovery
I achieve self-improvement on another level.
As I make things happen for myself, I become the catalyst
that makes things happen for those around me
I know who I am
and I am excited to be me.

Because I'm His

My relationship with my Heavenly Father
is uncompromising.
I am a lifetime member of the
fellowship of the unashamed.
I speak His Word, believe His Word,
trust His Word and will obey His Word.
I have the power to tread upon anything and everything
that is contrary to the promises of God for my life.
I refuse to give the enemy any air time
for his suggestions.
I say what God says regarding any situation
rather than speaking what I see.
I am steadfast and un-moveable, always abounding
in the work of the Lord.
I have on the whole armor of God.
I stand and withstand any onslaught,
because no weapon formed against me
will be able to prosper.
The battle is not mine,
the outcome has been pre-determined,
the Lord is on my side,
and I am victorious.

Celebrating Me

Today I celebrate who I am.
I have gifts and talents unique to me and me alone.
Others may be able to do what I do, but they
can only imitate my signature
in the way it is done.
I celebrate my abilities,
regardless of anyone else's comfort level.
I am motivated to express overwhelming gratitude
for what has been placed in me.
I have settled within myself
that I am a pattern. I am an original and
I am daily discovering "greater",
because of what has been placed in me.
I give time and attention to those I choose to include
in the future chapters of the book of my life.
I use every gift and talent I have
to be who and what I am created to be.
Yes, today is a day for celebration!

Character Traits

I am fearless because I am not alone.
I am supported by the hand of
the omnipotent, omniscient, omnipresent God.
I am anointed, appointed,
and blessed to be the best.
I am more than a conqueror
following God's guidance and direction.
Following the example of my Heavenly Father
I am forgiving, patient, kind, and I am available
for Kingdom work through Kingdom authority.
I have better than some and
more than most, but either way I am content.
I live an abundant life orchestrated by a sovereign God.
I am in my season and it shows.
I have Kingdom character and that gives me
reason to have a praise party
all by myself.

Chosen

I am chosen for a divine appointment
in the cabinet of the Kingdom of God
I display Christ-like characteristics
in support of my Kingdom credentials.
I am a power broker with respect
to my Kingdom assignment.
I create calm in chaotic situations.
I pray effectual, fervent prayers,
fully expecting my prayers to be answered
as I pray according to His Word.
I declare and decree
my expectation is elevated; anticipation is activated;
and I am courageous.
I proclaim victory over every situation and circumstance,
because I am chosen to shift the atmosphere.
I am fearless, filled with faith, and destiny driven.
I communicate in confidence
with the power of the Holy Spirit and
the authority of the Word of God
knowing what I say is so!

Confession of The Extraordinary

I refuse to be average
when I've been created to be extraordinary.
Everything intended for my life is beyond the norm.
What I accomplish will surpass the mediocre.
Good enough is on a lower level of my expectations.
I strive for and achieve excellence in my endeavors.
I see my end and it is bigger and better than my beginning.
I set new standards and
raise the bar on those already established.
I am inspired by the mountain.
I am encouraged by overcoming obstacles.
I am changed in the midst of the challenges.
The book of my life is still being written,
and each chapter
is more engaging and
more powerful than the one before.
I declare and decree it to be a best seller
in the genre of possibility publications.

Connection

I show respect to all who cross my path.
I treat others the way I want to be treated,
with kindness and love.
I recognize that just as I have purpose and dreams,
so do others.
Just as I experience pain, so do they.
Just as I have days that find me in the midst of storms,
so does everyone else.
I have empathy for someone's struggles.
I put myself in someone else's shoes and broaden my
ability to extend grace and show compassion.
I appreciate the value of each individual
and speak words of encouragement
into the lives of those I encounter.
Realizing I am part of something much greater
than my current situation,
my connection with others is purposeful
for them and for me.
I am the difference maker and my impact
is evident in the earth.

Essential to The Equation

Whatever I put my hands to will carry my uniqueness.
Since I am a one-of-a-kind design,
my creativity unlocks the same attributes that I possess
in all aspects of my life.
I am honored that I am imitated
because I matter, and I am essential to the equation of life.
I am fearless, courageous, and ultimately victorious
in my undertakings because I believe in me.
I speak things into existence and my conversations
convey only positive outcomes.
I am invited into circles of influence and
sought after by the influential.
I am prosperous in more than my bank account.
I have favor that surpasses my finances.
I have strength that ultimately eliminates any struggle.
I am a resource that will be instrumental in
the fulfillment of someone else's dream
and that will, in turn, accelerate my own.
Greatness is in me and will flow from me
as I make my mark
for the Kingdom.

Expansion

I expect expansion as I endeavor
to build extraordinary businesses
and business connections.
My reputation of operating with Christ-centered ethics is
woven into the fabric of the companies I represent.
My deliverables are distributed with confidence
because I am the best at what I am called to do
in my area of expertise.
Since I possess a passion for what I set out to accomplish,
my enthusiasm will create a ripple effect
for new opportunities to flow in my direction.
I have divine wisdom that enables me
to make divine decisions
that position me for a place of prominence
ahead of my competitors.
I expect money to come to me now and I shall have it.
I set my intentions for my partnerships
and collaborations to bring
growth and unlimited possibilities.
I win in the marketplace and my good success is inevitable
because that is who I am,
and this is what I do.

Forgiveness

To forgive
is one of the most important decisions I will ever make.
I realize and recognize forgiveness is for me.
I grow because of it.
I am strengthened by it.
I am wiser when I exercise it.
I am more powerful when I embody it.
I experience and enjoy true freedom in life
on a higher level
because I choose to forgive.
As the Father has forgiven me,
I forgive others with the same grace and
the same mercy that I have been afforded.
I forgive with love… in love…
and without hesitation and God gets the glory.
I exercise my God given right
to choose to forgive
and joy fills my soul.

Game Plan

I release the pains of the past and
embrace the possibilities in my future.
There is a time limit on my tears
and an expiration date on my fears.
Both have been identified, both will be followed
and freedom from that bondage is assured.
I declare and decree
I am in control of my emotions and
remain in a healthy place.
I know when enough is enough,
when too much is too much, and
when just enough is more than enough.
Now that I know I am stronger
than I once perceived,
I am in pursuit of what belongs to me
and I will recover all.

Health is Mine

I focus on my health daily
and boldly declare and decree that
sickness and disease are far from me.
I am designed to walk in supernatural health, therefore
every cell in my body must line up to perfection,
every muscle and every joint
moving properly and
operating the way they were intended.
If I am faced with a difficult diagnosis,
I believe the report of the Lord.
I affirm that by His stripes I am already healed.
As I allow this divine healing to overtake my body
pain must be evicted.
I eat properly. I exercise regularly.
I rest to be re-energized, refreshed, renewed and restored.
I have work to do and a race to run
and I am determined to finish the course
healthy and whole.

I Am A Gift

I have something to offer the world.
My gift is making room for me and
huge doors are opening on my behalf.
As a gift, I am a finisher, submitted to the process
for the manifestation of my purpose
to love, to give,
to encourage, and to bless.
I am a gift courageous in crisis, authentic in adversity, and
triumphant even in the midst of tragedy.
I am priceless, therefore misuse and abuse
are removed from how I am treated.
I declare and decree, I am a gift from God,
to be used by God,
for the plans of God
and I am to be forever treasured.

Income and Increase

I have gifts and talents that enable me to create
multiple streams of income.
God prospers the work of my hands.
Everyone I encounter knows what I do.
Every transaction will ultimately be for His glory
and allow me to be a blessing to someone else.
I operate with the spirit of an entrepreneur continuously.
People seeking my goods and services will find me,
ready, willing, and able to assist.
I am known for business principles and practices
that are governed by honesty and integrity.
I speak blessings over those who pray with me and for me,
and are fervent in fulfilling their assignment.
I accept rejection and delays as temporary situations,
understanding every 'no' brings me closer to the God-intended 'yes.'
I am encouraged because I know
wealth belongs to me.
God has enlarged my capacity and I am ready for increase.

Lessons Learned

The lessons I have learned from past mistakes
are positioning me for future victories.
Dwelling on victories is productive
to the destiny designed for my life.
My energy is driving me to focus on what will be
rather than what has been,
because better is the end of a thing
than the beginning thereof.
I apply lessons learned and
I develop strategies to ensure I accelerate
the pursuit of corrective action.
I am prepared to embrace the learning process
and accept it for what it is,
a catalyst for success.
Therefore, I am better, stronger,
more enlightened, and more empowered,
because of lessons learned.

Love Is

My love walk is apparent in everything I undertake.
It dictates my words, my actions, and my reactions
as I exemplify the love of God.
I care for others as I do for myself,
making it easy for me to consider someone else's needs
as if they were my own.
As I love, I look for the best
without keeping score of the sins of others.
I uplift others when they are weary and encourage them to
be the best that they can be.
I look at things through the lens of love
without envy, jealousy, or spite.
I keep going, continuing to look ahead.
That is what love is.
That is what love does.
I do what I do because of love,
trusting God always
without expectation of anything in return.
I am fulfilled because
my love walk is strong.

My Identity

I am the handiwork of God
and He is mindful of me.
He has plans for me that must come to pass,
because nothing can stop
predestinated plans of God for my life – nothing!
I walk in victory knowing
God is working all things together for my good.
I walk in peace and gratitude
with a blessed assurance,
for God is faithful.
Everything about me reflects the light and love of Christ,
regardless of my present circumstance.
I create calm in the midst of confusion.
The anointing of God gives me power.
I am someone's blessing by divine appointment.
I am worship… I am praise… I am a prayer warrior…
and I am indeed fearfully and wonderfully made.
I am a chosen child of the Most High God
and He is pleased with His design.

My Path

Today I am refreshed and ready to reset if necessary.
I am determined to be proactive and productive
in order to accomplish the goals I have set before me.
I am analyzing my assignments,
considering my commitments,
adjusting my goals,
and revisiting my timelines to ensure
they are feasible and realistic.
Since I have conquered procrastination,
I am on track, on time,
and gaining an exemplary reputation
for my integrity, accountability, and dependability.
I know how to encourage myself
to maintain my motivation and
move forward in my purpose.
I am destined for greatness, following my path of purpose,
and what I affirm shall come to pass.

Predestinated

I have been bought with a price
and I am in the earth to do the will of
my Heavenly Father.
Committed and submitted, I surrender all.
I acknowledge God in all my ways
and allow Him to direct my path.
Divine appointments have already been set for me today
and I am equipped to handle every one.
I was predestinated as an ambassador for the Kingdom.
The light and love of Christ in me
emanates from me and
causes someone to ask,
"What must I do to be saved?"
Before the foundation of the world,
everything was placed in me that I would ever need
to be able to be who I am called to be and
do exquisitely what I am called to do.
I am blessed.

Prosperity Plan

I declare and decree, prosperity is the result
of every good thing I endeavor to accomplish.
I refuse to accept limitations as a way of life.
While increase is found in areas
other than the form of finances,
my bank accounts prove I am a lender and not a borrower
with financial strategies to keep me in overflow.
My prayer life continuously increases,
enabling me to quickly
tap into God's guidance and direction for my destiny.
My circle of influence includes productive people of power.
My unique creativity gives me an edge for success.
My awareness of stumbling blocks keeps me
on my path of purpose
to recognize, realize, and receive
the best life has to offer.
Since I have the power to get wealth,
my prosperity plan is in operation,
and wealth will manifest.

Ready to Receive

I am ready for increase and overflow.
"Idle" is my enemy and productivity is my ally.
Everything that I do from this day forward
is done with purpose in mind.
I set attainable goals for my life.
I am intentional in my preparation
for those goals to be realized.
Stretching beyond my comfort zone
is a requirement for my destiny.
Thinking outside of the box
is a prerequisite for my dreams.
I parlay whatever I find on my path,
whether it is good or bad,
into an opportunity for growth and advancement.
Whether portfolio or people,
I receive a return for every seed I sow
and every investment I make because
God will bless me indeed and enlarge my territory.
The strategies I implement give me the capacity I need
so I am ready to receive.

Right Relationships

I am blessed with healthy relationships.
I have decided that it is imperative
that relationships with me
are reciprocal,
which keeps feelings of being used or abused
from entering into the equation.
My relationships are loving and strong because their
foundation
is based on honor, respect, and integrity.
I enter in cautiously, but with an open mind
refusing to hold present relationships
hostage to past experiences.
I welcome like minds, as well as those who challenge me
to grow, broaden my perspective,
and be open to change.
I recognize right relationships that lift me up,
and willingly release those
that are detrimental to my destiny.
I declare and decree,
my relationships are precious, positive, purposeful,
and enhance this journey called
my life.

Setting the Day In Motion

I am confident as I greet the day
that it will be extraordinary.
Because I know who and whose I am,
my thoughts are clear and precise.
I receive divine downloads that
determine the direction of my dreams.
Whatever is ahead of me
is to build me up for the blessings intended just for me.
Any delay I experience is only an indicator
that what I am about to receive
is greater than I could ever
think or imagine.
I am strengthened by the acknowledgment that
I am a work in progress being perfectly positioned
for my purpose.
I am clothed in the full armor of God and
I am ready for the day.

Submitted to Him

I am subject to the Lordship of Christ.
My mind is stayed on Him and His plan for my life.
I operate in faith, believing and trusting the God I serve
rather than what I see.
I am successful and prosperous because
that is God's will for my life.
I am abundantly blessed and daily loaded with benefits.
Favor and increase are divinely ordered for my life.
I am enlarged daily so that
I have the capacity to receive
the abundant, pressed down, shaken together and
running over blessings with my name on them.
I am submitted to His will
and obedient to His Word.
I yield to the power and authority of my
Lord and Savior
I have exchanged my agenda
for His agenda and my life is better because of it.
Now I walk in victory.

This Is the Day

This is the day that the Lord has made
I will rejoice and be glad in it.
The joy of the Lord is my strength
Yes, I am strong in the Lord and the power of His might.
I allow Jesus-joy to permeate every situation and
circumstance
in my life as I seek the face of my Father
before I ever seek His hand.
I consult my advocate, Jesus Christ,
in all situations and
draw from the well of the power within me.
His path is the one I follow.
His voice is the one I hear.
His Word is the word I believe.
Broken places have been mended,
condemnation is rescinded,
enemies befriended,
because this is the day that the Lord has made.
I rejoice, and I am glad in it!

Thoughts

I only think on those things that are positive, purposeful
and bring encouragement to my soul.
Since my thoughts control my words.
I declare and decree only good things so that
my words bring life.
I think of opportunities rather than obstacles;
prosperity rather than poverty;
peace rather than problems;
strength rather than sickness;
dreams rather than disappointments;
success rather than shortcomings;
abundance rather than inadequacy;
and above all
I think myself happy!
I walk in power and strength because
my thoughts are grounded in His Word
and in accordance to His will.

Transformation

I have moved from the land of limitation
on the outskirts of opportunity.
I am at home in the province of possibilities.
I live a limitless life filled with desires that are attainable
because of the Christ in me.
When I stand up, God stands up.
When I speak, God speaks through me.
I do what I do under the unction of the Holy Spirit.
I follow the path God has already laid out for me.
I am set apart and in right standing with my Creator.
When people look at me,
they see the Christ in me and
immediately know that I am His.
I am a change agent and a difference maker
capable of shifting the atmosphere.
All that I have and all that I am is because
I am transformed by the renewing of my mind.

Traveling Light

I am unpacking the baggage of my past
to move into my future.
I travel light in order to shift at any moment.
I only carry the necessary emotional luggage
to ensure I have space available for
lessons learned that need to be remembered.
I leave behind anything contrary to the promises of God.
Instead I am taking my love, anticipation,
expectation, confidence,
positive memories, feelings of forgiveness,
and my faith.
I am packing my praise and protecting my purpose.
I have a date with destiny
and I will be on time.

Turnaround

I am experiencing the turnaround of my life.
My mind is renewed.
I am stronger than I have ever been.
I shift quicker than I ever could.
I have so much favor resting on my life that
my enemies bless me without even understanding why.
What was intended to extinguish the flames of my passion
ignites fires of motivation and inspiration so
I excel and exceed.
Understanding has taken up residence where
preconceived notions used to reside.
Positive seeds of harmony, truth,
and love have been planted
and changed the landscape of my life.
All things are turning around,
working together for my good
and contributing to the transformation process.
Now I rejoice and move from mountaintop,
to mountaintop,
to mountaintop…

Whose I Am

I am my Father's child.
I carry the DNA of my Daddy,
Abba Father,
and I am joint heir with Jesus.
I declare and decree that peace is mine,
prosperity is mine,
unmerited favor is mine,
endless increase is mine,
power is mine,
joy is mine,
strength is mine,
It is evident in my countenance and
in my conversation that
I live a life of abundance and overflow.
Unmistakably, undeniably
I am my Father's child
and for that reason
I am a benefactor of the blessings of the Lord.

Now, It's Your Turn!

I hope you have gained inspiration through the affirmations you have been reading. If you've made the decision to be more aware of communicating in a positive manner and more deliberate in avoiding words that project negativity, these next pages are for you. Take the time to create your own powerful affirmations. I've included a page for thirty-one days. It may not be easy at first, but it is worth it. When you are cognizant of your conversation you will be amazed at how quickly you are able to adjust your mood and your attitude. A sentence will shift the atmosphere and a phrase will reposition your thought process to tap into the power within. Take control, think with intent, write with authority so when life speaks, you'll speak life!

Day One

Day Two

Day Three

Day Four

Day Five

Day Six

Day Seven

Day Eight

Day Nine

Day Ten

Day Eleven

Day Twelve

Day Thirteen

Day Fourteen

Day Fifteen

Day Sixteen

Day Eighteen

Day Nineteen

Day Twenty

Day Twenty-One

Day Twenty-Two

Day Twenty-Three

Day Twenty-Four

Day Twenty-Five

Day Twenty-Six

Day Twenty-Seven

Day Twenty-Eight

Day Twenty-Nine

Day Thirty

Day Thirty-One

Acknowledgments

When you have celebrated as many anniversaries of being in receipt of your AARP card as I have, you realize it is impossible to name every person who has had an impact on your life. For me, the friendships God has blessed me to sustain; my family, natural and extended, that encourage and support in their own way; the acquaintances that have made me stronger by their presence or their absence; the divine appointments of chance encounters that have birthed verses that inspire others; every one that has crossed my path falls into one of these categories. Each category has been a vital part of my growth and development. I may not be able to name all of you, but I thank each of you for whatever role you played. The names I will mention here in no way suggest that others are not important. While I can't tell it all, I must add that I am deeply grateful for the maturity of those not mentioned who will continue to be secure in their place in my life and their contribution to my accomplishments. But there has been something so unique in my relationship with the following people I needed them, and you, to receive my acknowledgment of who they are and the difference they have made in my journey.

Pastor Sheryl and Bishop Joby Brady, for pouring a foundational relationship with Christ so strong that I continue to build upon it with unshakeable, unmovable, immeasurable gratitude.

Bishop Ronald L. Godbee, Sr. and Pastor Karla Godbee, whose genuine love, support, and kindness have given me courage and strength to continue with confidence.

Pastors Steve and Valarie Sims, whose display of integrity

and Kingdom character keep me encouraged and mindful that the prayers of the righteous availeth much.

Thank you "Tracy Mac", for creating a safe place for my truth and demonstrating that business and personal relationships can intersect producing power and peace.

Cinnamon Ruth Leggett, for nudging me out of procrastination into profound productivity.

Ruth Griffin, for the understanding and guidance given to each project, enabling me to birth His words and prayerfully touch the world.

My gratitude is limitless…

About the Author

Andrea L. Hines
*Mother, Grandmother, Author, Poet, Speaker,
Entrepreneur, Doctor of Divinity, Certified Life Coach
and Radio Host*

This lady of many talents is a native of Washington, D.C. who now resides in Raleigh, NC. She often says that moving to the "quiet beauty of the Carolinas" deepened her relationship with God and caused her creativity to flow freely."

Andrea has over thirty years of experience in the performing arts as an actor, playwright and director, with work including performances in numerous community theatre and film projects. She has been a narrator for the North Carolina Library for the Blind and Physically Handicapped; and continues to enjoy lending her voice to any number of voice-over projects.

Her poetic work has been featured in local newspapers, on Blue Mountain Arts greeting cards and products, and included in numerous anthologies. She has written a collection of inspirational verses titled 'When He Whispers', and words of encouragement inspired by her granddaughter titled, 'Nanny Nuggets'. While Andrea has authored story poems, greeting cards and other works, she says God has given her the ability to write the words people often think but can't express.

She introduced her company, A's Accents in 1994. Her performance and product showcase, "...A Work in Progress.," weaves a story of life experiences through her original verses with musical interludes. "A Reading for His Glory" provides a more intimate atmosphere with smaller groups, giving them the opportunity to interact with the author on a more personal level. Her style and ability to uplift the heart has made her a favorite speaker in areas from commencement exercises to conferences. You can see her on her You Tube channel – Andrea L. Hines – and hear her as she hosts her own radio program WHEN LIFE

SPEAKS on the WOE Network Women of Essence radio and TV an affiliate of SIBN – Streaming Inspirational Broadcast Network. Andrea is also "the voice of the poet" on CYM radio.

Andrea has received an honorary Doctorate Degree of Divinity and is an Elder at River Church in Durham, NC. She is a Certified Life Coach, an affiliate of TRACYMAC Solutions for Life Institute, and owner of C.L.A.S.S Coaching and Consulting-Cultivating Lives and Success Strategies. She believes God has blessed her with certain gifts, and only hopes that whatever she creates will be to His glory and a blessing to someone else.

Find the Author Online

On Twitter: Hispen2

On Facebook: Andrea L Hines

On YouTube: Andrea L Hines

As a Radio Host for When Life Speaks on Facebook's WOE Network Women Of Essence Radio & Television

Via Email: alh@andrealhines.com

On the Web: andrealhines.com
(Effective October 15, 2018)

Also Available from the Author

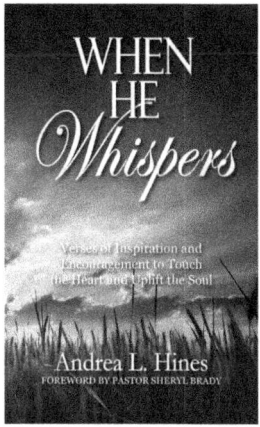

"I used to think God only spoke in a booming voice. I anticipated the earth would quake when He wanted to get my attention. You know, a "burning bush" experience. Instead, I find He loves to whisper to me in the quiet stillness of the early morning hours when it's just the two of us.

"Whether you are in a season of great success or a season of great struggle, you need to be encouraged from time to time.

"These specially selected verses from my time with Him are designed to speak to the heart and uplift the soul. Read them thoughtfully, cover to cover, or allow a title to catch your eye and ignite your curiosity. Either way, I pray you will allow His Words to touch you as only He can when He whispers!"

Also Available from the Author

Everyone needs to know that in spite of what they are going through, they matter! Self-esteem concerns, identity crisis, feelings of aloneness and being misunderstood – these are all issues everyone deals with, and if you're facing them now, then Nanny Nuggets are just what you need. A treasure chest of wisdom, these words will encourage you to redirect your focus, change your perspective, activate your faith, and begin again. Take a moment to read and be renewed. You won't regret it.

www.ingramcontent.com/pod-product-compliance
Lightning Source LLC
Chambersburg PA
CBHW071504070526
44578CB00001B/434